Table of Contents

Rourke
Educational Media

rourkeeducationalmedia.com

Can you find these words?

creativity

sidewalk

steps

strait

Golden Gate Bridge

A symbol stands for an idea.

The Golden Gate Bridge is in California.

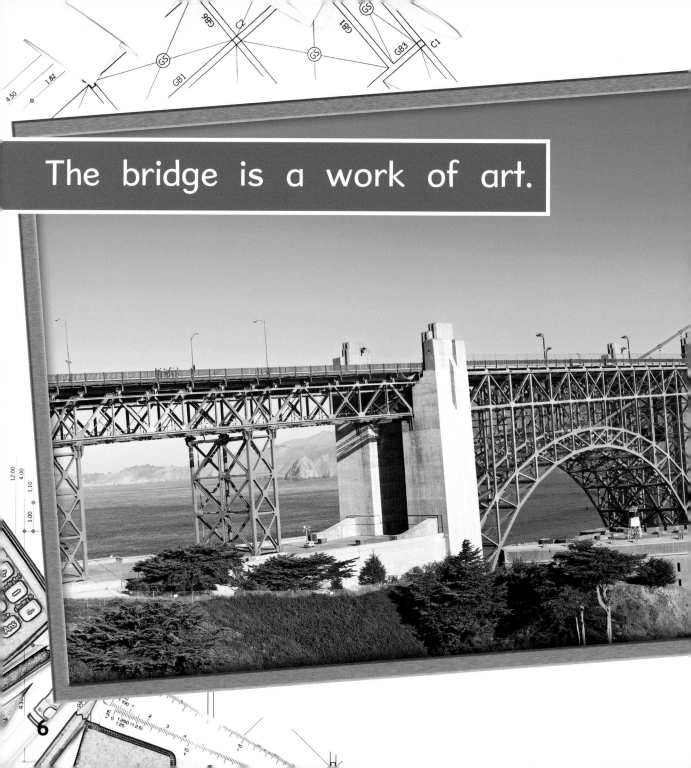

The bridge is a work of art.

It is a symbol of American **creativity**.
It is a symbol of skill.

It stretches across a body of water called a **strait**.

It is almost two miles
(three kilometers) long.

Almost
2 MILES LONG

That's about four thousand **steps!**

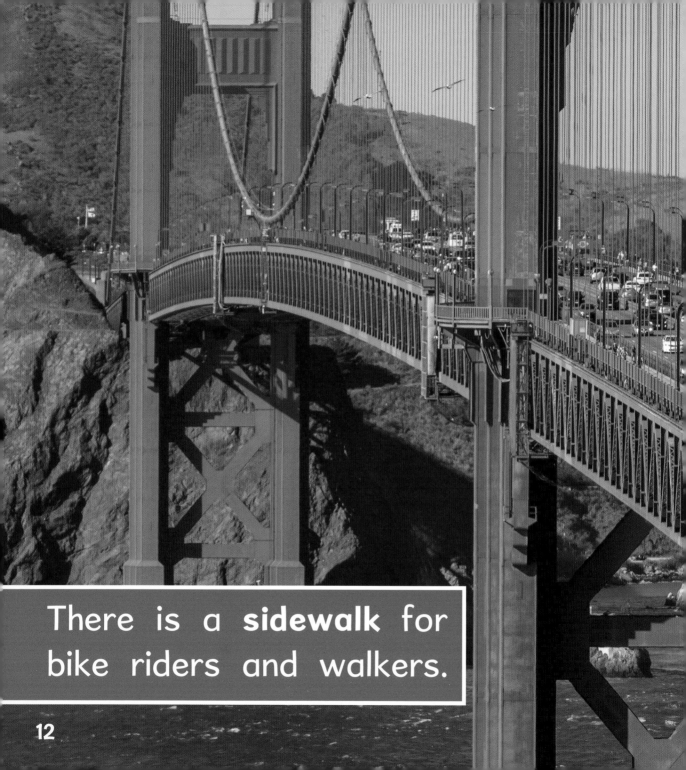

There is a **sidewalk** for bike riders and walkers.

Thousands of cars cross the bridge every day.

Did you find these words?

It is a symbol of American **creativity**.

There is a **sidewalk** for bike riders and walkers.

That's about four thousand **steps**!

It stretches across a body of water called a **strait**.

Photo Glossary

 **creativity** (kree-AY-tiv-uh-tee): The use of imagination and new ideas to create something.

 **sidewalk** (SIDE-wawk): A paved path that runs beside a street.

 **steps** (steps): The movements of your feet while walking, running, climbing, or dancing.

 **strait** (strayt): A narrow strip of water that connects two larger bodies of water.

Index

About the Author

K.A. Robertson is a writer and editor who enjoys learning about the history of the United States. She thinks the Golden Gate Bridge is beautiful.

www.rourkeeducationalmedia.com

PHOTO CREDITS: Cover: ©vicm; p2,7,14,15: ©fotoVoyager; p2,12,14,15: ©Spondylolithesis; p2,11,14,15: ©Ljupco, p2,8,14,15: ©blinx; p3: ©daniel rodriguez; p4: ©NicolasMcComber; p7: ©Adkasai; p10,11: ©Flightlevel80

Edited by: Keli Sipperley
Cover and interior design by: Kathy Walsh

Library of Congress PCN Data
Golden Gate Bridge / K.A. Robertson
(Visiting U.S. Symbols)
ISBN 978-1-64369-060-5 (hard cover)(alk. paper)
ISBN 978-1-64369-079-7 (soft cover)
ISBN 978-1-64369-207-4 (e-Book)
Library of Congress Control Number: 2018955840

Printed in the United States of America, North Mankato, Minnesota